FIVE INDISCRETIONS

D1291989

FIVE INDISCRETIONS

A Book of Poems

By

Alberto <u>Ríos</u>

The Sheep Meadow Press
Riverdale-on-Hudson, New York

ACKNOWLEDGMENTS

A number of these poems have appeared in the following journals and anthologies:

American Poetry Review, The Bilingual Review / La Revista Bilingue, The Black Warrior Review, Citybender, Ironwood, Mango, New Kauri, Northeast Journal, The Occasional Review, The Ohio Review, Pearl, Poetasumanos, Whetstone, Window Rock, Agua Fresca, *and* Backward Dancer.

PS
3568
.I587
F5
1985

© 1985 Alberto Ríos. All rights reserved. Published 1985

Printed in the United States of America

The Sheep Meadow Press, Riverdale-on-Hudson, N.Y.

Typesetting by Keystrokes, Lenox, Massachusetts

Distributed by Persea Books
225 Lafayette Street
New York, N.Y. 10012

Library of Congress Cataloging in Publication Data

Ríos, Alberto
  Five Indiscretions
    84-052616
ROO 65726606 /
ISBN 0-935296-57-3
ISBN 0-935296-58-1 (pbk.)

Café Combate, ¡la gente toma!
Café Combate, ¡de rica aroma!

—a famous, and old, commercial jingle run
on the radio in Mexico for many years,
advertising a particular brand of coffee.
It ran repeatedly, obsessively, and no
one who heard it has been able to forget.

Café Combate, the people drink it!
Café Combate, such rich aroma!

CONTENTS

One

Two

Three

Four

One

Taking Away the Name of a Nephew

One of the disappeared looks like this:
One shirt, reasonable shoes, no laces, no face
Recognizable even to the mother of this thing.
Lump. Dropped egg, bag of old potatoes
Too old and without moisture, a hundred eyes
Sprouted out and gone wild into forest
Food for the maggot flies and small monsters.
Bag. Pulled by the tiestring
The laces around his ankles have become.
A crisp bag of seventeen birthdays
Six parties with piñatas and the particular
Memory of a thick hugging
His Tía Susí gave him with the strong arms
Her breasts were, how they had held him
Around his just-tall-enough throat and had reached
To touch each other behind his neck.

His memory of Susí was better than how the soldier held him
She hoped this out of all things.
That she had made him warm.
In that body the three soldiers were fooled, tricked
A good hundred strings of wool put over their eyes:
They did not take away the boy.
They took away his set of hands and his spine
Which in weeks would look like railroad tracks
Along the side of any young mountain.
One of the disappeared looks like this
The newspaper said. She had seen
The photograph which looked like all
Newspaper photographs,
Had thought it does not say *looked* like this,

But *looks* like this, still; had thought
What is being said here is that he did not die.
It was not death that took him.

She thinks about things like this, this way:
Here is the new mathematics made simple
Here is the algebra I once did not understand.
She sets for herself the tasks of a student,
Making clear the equations
Breathing the air that Einstein breathed.
She looks in her purse and pulls out three coins.
This much for one dozen corn tortillas. Easy.
A paper cut, small slice, magnified three times:
$PC \times 3 =$
This is what a very small Newberry's letter opener—
A gift from her cousin in the United States—
Held as a knife at the stomach of a man
Then pushed in, this is what it might feel like.
Stomachache from a winter's flu, the rocking kind
During which one must hold and bite a towel
Or those first days womanhood finds its way
Shaking her with pains, magnified three times, also:
This must be what the beginnings of a cancer
Feel like, how one's hands can do nothing
More than rub, or clean, or stroke the forehead,
Cannot in a last, most desperate attempt
Go out into the alley behind the bar like the men
And try to beat it up.

She thinks about this like this:
Then she stops, because she can
Understand a paper cut and stomach flu
As she understands salt and bread,
Can imagine them even together, and eating them.

4

She stops because understanding the blossom
Pain must be, or more,
That pain is a blossom snapped off
That móment and the pungent smell
A long *o* sound makes in the mouth
On a face not big enough—
All this disallows the thinking of a thing for too long
Because one understands.
All this stops the reading of newspapers.
But some nights she cannot do otherwise, as tonight:
She begins to add up, again, to put numbers
In the equation of how many cuts and glowing scrapes
One more thing or another adds up to,
What it must feel like,
How many paper cuts might roughly equal
The breaking neck of a favorite nephew.

Her Dream is of the Sea

Women on boats at night in winter
walk along the fine wide decks
walk on the magnificent wood come from trees
staid a hundred years in an Oregon forest
waiting their time for this, a woman's foot.
The women walk in ten-rabbit coats
brocades and cigarette-holders,
they walk, and comment on the walk
the night and the winter, comment on
the particular arrangement of the sky
tonight, how the angles of Orion
remind this certain darling Mariquita of roses,
how sixteen roses once stood in bloom
a surprise in the center of her table.
Darling Mariquita of the night tonight
goes in to dine, to dance, then to sleep.

Her dream is this: the same as it has been.
Her dream is of the sea, liquid, gelatinous almost
skinless body held fat by the thousand salts
that retain water, so much salt
that the water, even from a skinless body, cannot escape.
But it tries, it moves and it heaves
ready and ready like unshaven men with tattoos preparing
in that way they do to move a piano.
The tides are shoulders flexing
or the process of food coming up from the stomach.
One day the sea will do it, she imagines,
a real, green and gray and large upthrowing
of doubloons and penises,
fishheads and pork. She wakes

6

and in the dimmed light sees her hand,
only her hand, how
cut off in this way of the dark from her arm
it looks like a starfish,
the severed hands of drowned sailors
her grandmother had said, but no
it was not that quite.
Starfish, hands connected to the women
who had thought over their suicides
then changed their minds but too late.

The Bath

The woman undressed
and put her nipples on
for decoration
so as to bathe lavishly.
She kept them in the water
next to her bed
where the teeth had been
years ago.
She floated in the water
watching her skin fold
again then again.
These were the treasures,
the only heirlooms left,
and she guarded them
now, like diamond earrings.
She thought as she looked
that she would like very much
to be buried with them on.
Slowly they float from
her body going off like boats
onto the water.

A Dream of Husbands

Though we thought it, Doña Carolina did not die.
She was too old for that nonsense, and too set.
That morning she walked off just a little farther
into her favorite dream, favorite but not nice
so much, not nice and not bad, so it was not death.
She dreamed the dream of husbands
and over there she found him after all the years.
Cabrón, she called him, *animal,* very loud
so we could hear it, for us it was a loud truck
passing, or thunder, or too many cats, very loud
for having left her for so long and so far. Days now
her voice is the squeak of the rocking chair
as she complains, we hear it, it will not go
not with oils or sanding or shouts back at her.
But it becomes too the sound a spoon makes, her old
very large wooden spoon as it stirs a pot of soup.
Dinnertimes, we think of her, the good parts, of her
cooking, we like her best then, even the smell of her.
But then, *cabrones* she calls us, *animales,* irritated,
from over there, from the dream, they come, her words
they are the worst sounds of the street in the night
so that we will not get so comfortable about her,
so comfortable with her having left us
we thinking that her husband and her long dream
are so perfect, because no, they are not, not so much,
she is not so happy this way, not in this dream,
this is not heaven, don't think it. She tells us this,
sadness too is hers, a half measure, sadness at having
no time for the old things, for rice, for chairs.

9

The Night a Daughter Goes Away

She imagines the perfect braid on her thin back
as the hand of a young boy, his whole arm,
and she nods her head, *yes,* fully up and down
when the questions in school are asked of her,
feels him soothing her, trying just her, only her,
yes when she reads quickly the paperback books,
yes nodding as she agrees with her sad mother
about how she will behave and what the world is.
A third hand when the newest winter has come
and the cold, and the clothes to try and cover up,
a third hand keeping her more warm than sweaters,
trying sometimes with all of its quick fingers
to go farther, to get around her, to suddenly fall
instead on the small front of her new body
when she leans for water or at dinner, or church
at the moment when she is most quiet, kneeling.
But she takes those fingers fast in her own,
shushes them back as cats from the side door
until they stay where she decides they must,
this boy trying only sometimes to be stronger
than her other two hands, this cousin Julio
with strong legs and lines drawn on them,
this René whose eyes she imagines as the darkest
night ever in this world, that singular, that much
like Queretaro and the opals, that much
like fire and the color of what it touches,
but this one boy with his eyes and his strong
strong legs waits for her to be very tired
one night, whispers her long name from behind
this night, as she sits alone on a padded chair.

Prayers to the Dangerous

Pretty girls go walking away to prayers.
What they pray for, C-shaped, is not so different:
homemade waffles, omelettes all filled with mushrooms.
But in the omelettes
one girl thinks of fire: in his hands, and eyelids
as they drooped, that halfway excruciation
coming from a moment without a name yet,
pressing and pressing.

Boy. You never told me about the burning
fires you'd leave inside, how an inside's burning
makes a blackness there, and the black is empty,
charred like a night's sky,
sky the sun has burnt and then left, with embers
there instead of stars, like the Elks Club picnic
finished, charcoal stars as the only warm things
drunk men can talk to.
Danger boy, you could have remembered my skin.
I remember you, how I swallowed tender
words you had inside, on your tongue, all water.
Hands, how they touched me . . .

C-shaped on her pew, in that lean of children praying,
one girl only dreams of the ripest berries,
undersides of mushrooms, that color, pepper.
These are her prayers:
how, as food, she wishes for him, his touching.
That his fire leaves a black in her mouth, her eyes, her
fisted hands, means a place for his returning.
These are her prayers.

Advice to a First Cousin

The way the world works is like this:
for the bite of scorpions, she says,
my grandmother to my first cousin,
because I might die and someone must know,
go to the animal jar
the one with the soup of green herbs
mixed with the scorpions I have been putting in
still alive. Take one out
put it on the bite. It has had time to think
there with the others—put the lid back tight—
and knows that a biting is not the way to win
a finger or a young girl's foot.
It will take back into itself the hurting
the redness and the itching and its marks.

But the world works like this, too:
look out for the next scorpion you see,
she says, and makes a big face to scare me
thereby instructing my cousin, look out!
for one of the scorpion's many
illegitimate and unhappy sons.
It will be smarter, more of the devil.
It will have lived longer than these dead ones.
It will know from them something more
about the world, in the way mothers know
when something happens to a child, or how
I knew from your sadness you had been bitten.
It will learn something stronger than biting.
Look out most for that scorpion, she says,

making a big face to scare me again and it works
I go—crying—she lets me go—they laugh,
the way you must look out for men
who have not yet bruised you.

Her Second Weight

She was stretched on the ground
for the first time by a man
the year of the three summers,
the year she felt for the first time
a heat in her stomach and ankles.
Today she thought of that man again
and could remember his real name
which was the feel of his large face,
how it scratched, and hurt her,
how the first time she had seen
a forest of pine trees from the top
she had also thought of him,
how the scratching points of these trees
had stuck into her too well,
had almost stayed there in her face
like a hook absolute to a fish.
She remembered his mouth,
how it had wanted her,
how it had tried to open wide enough
for her to step into
and how his hands could not stop
their work, which was the work of bees,
the humming and the making of sugars.
And after he had lain on her and gotten up
the weight of his body did not go,
only his name walked from her.
And when she got up from under the trees
herself, how strong this being able
to rise made her feel, that she could
get up with the weight of his body
still on her, how sure and combed

14

this walking away by herself, how light
this second weight that she carried
in the many lids of her eyes.

Perhaps Harder Contours

Each Saturday without fail
she cast off her burden by confessing.
Her pursuant devotions were as a canvas
done by the miracle painters who worked
with shadows, and she was pretty in them
as if Catholicism were her natural breath
the way she imagined when she was young
and had the cats and the water and herself blessed.
But her irritability now came also in a dim light
yet in a different place, and when she was alone,
and it formed then more than an inch thick inside,
in herself too much almost to fit there.

And the door to the bedroom would lift
off its hinges altogether, but no one would come.
Finally she would lay herself face down, tight
on her soft man and pull the imaginary eel
like a rope, a man's rope, around and around her
so that all but the most precisely vital
parts of her could no longer move, not one move.
She wore only sandals in her bed
to balance the weight she felt behind her eyes.
And then she moved those other parts of herself
which had no face. This was the signal to begin
an even harder and more dangerous week.

The Women at Early Mass

Small towns have the smell,
wood burning, cool air,
houses high on the sides
of painted small mountains,
silent smell that stands
arms folded and thick

as a man's are thick.
Small towns know the smell
no one understands.
One man dreams it as the air
half strong in the mountains,
young girls on their sides

propped and nude, white sides
exposed, breasts as thick
and sloped as new mountains
whose smooth, hard pine smell
braids now the rented air
where a thin girl stands

ashamed for him, and he stands,
but still dreams, so his sides
stay as pained as the red air
that moment is thick
suddenly; and the smell
of pain is also mountains

in wives, whose mountains
never were, Wife, who stands
the thin sexual smell
of his dreams, who sides
with this man grown thick,
strong, high in the air

but then sad—that air,
the weight of mountains,
is always more thick
than himself. She stands
pain too in her sides:
the fat, votive smell

of white air; she too stands
beneath mountains, with sides
thick, but scrubbed of smell.

The Birthday of Mrs. Pineda

Maria Pineda, about to tell the story of Anna's visit and wrestling around very quickly in her head for extra words to make the story better and so to keep his tender and old attention longer, saw Adolfo Pineda smile at her.

Just smile at her.

He had not done that, not like that, since before, since the far before. He still smiled at her, but his smiles were embers now, not strong quick wood fires. They were warmer now, and most lasting, but his smiles no longer held a sense of danger, that they might burn, that they might reach off his face and stretch in some lightning bolt fist straight at her, down and through the electricity in the cells at the core of her inside self.

She had been Maria Elena then, daughter of the vendor of strings, strings for all occasions, and rough cotton threads, Don Miguel, and his wife, la señora Beltran, who never smiled and so was never addressed by her first name.

But her Fito was smiling at her now, and she was standing in the time when he had called her by the names of various imported perfumes taken, he would say, from the wildest flowers of the wilted and perfect bouquets found in subtle crystal vases set on absurd tables in one particular back street bistro in springtime Paris just the year before.

He said this, but it said nothing about what he would do. From that moment she could never disentwine her other memory of the time of perfumes, that time just after they had married when she had to go looking for him, had to step over a dried phlegm and dirt floor in a dark cock-fighting barn, had to step over this floor made of sputum from half-shaved, thick men and dying cocks, a floor bloodstained and scuffed into a kind of inexpert, misshapen

19

setting of scab tiles. The sounds of the fight would not go away, the sounds of all those men huddled, nor the odor of that perfume, and she remembered how she had seen as she ran by the one soul-white cock splattered with blood like grease, hot, how it had an eye pulled clean out but continued to fight, and then lost the other eye, but continued to fight, stretching its head and neck up higher and higher imagining that something must be blocking its view, trying to see, and trying higher to see, but never for a moment thinking that it was blind. The owners kept spraying the fighter birds with water from their mouths, spitting a mist, cooling and cooling, fooling them, until the winner, the not-white one, allowed itself to be cooled and soothed and rewarded, and the owner, who was laughing, took its head into his mouth, cooling him.

Maria Pineda ran by them all, that perfume, into the rooms behind the barn, into one room of particular use, and she pulled Adolfo Pineda physically out of another woman and dragged him drunk home.

Five Indiscretions,

or The Unfortunate Story of the Unmarried Flora Carrillo
And the Man Who Loved Her Before He Died his Famous Death,
From Whose Single Liaison a Daughter Was Born
And the Advice, Rather the Explanation,
Both of Them Left for Her, And the Story Also
Of What She Became, and That She Was Happy

1.
Three did not count.
A fourth was forgiven by the Father Torres
In exchange for reasonable payment,
Two full days of the Hail Mary.
Bigger than priests, the fifth
Indiscretion was born on a Thursday, early
Evening in a November not too cold.
No rain had fallen
And the birds had not yet gone.
She chose a black dress, this Flora, Florita

+ here evoke the names of saints +

Underneath which she carried tonight
An old blade, but of fine Toledo forging
Long as the member of this man
In love with this woman standing at his door.
Her head was filled with the vines of the jungle
The noises of a lion, the feel of ten birds
Trying with their beaks to get out.
All anger: that she had hoped he would
Come to her bedroom.

And that he had.

     Faster than !that she took from him his rolled tongue
Hanging there between his thin legs, his two-fingers,
This girl's wrist and fist of his
Its central tendon and skin that moved on itself,
This small and second body of his
Which had found its way to her second mouth,
This part of himself which he had given her
Then taken back on this same day, earlier
His ugly afternoon of loving her too much.
He would scream as she had
When she had taken him in first as a leg-bone
And held him there too long, too much
Until he had become a pinky-finger

    + here evoke the holy names +

Which she !took now and put in the dowry
She would make for her new daughter.
With it she would write a note,
Nothing else was left to do:
> *Daughter, you will be an only child.*
> *The story of your birth will smell on you.*
> *Do this: take baths filled with rosemary*
> *With leaves, with pinched orange peels.*
> *Keep secret the fact of yourself.*
> *Be happy enough, happy with this much life.*
> *Ask for nothing. Do not live for a long time.*

2.

He sang to her the oldest song
That he was a piccolo flute in the small of her heart
Or, if that were not convincing, too much filled with flowers,

A small noise, then, a smart, a cut which is healing
Its face feeling good to be scratched
The way even wild cats like;
A piccolo flute in the small of her heart
Nothing more, and nothing more necessary
A noise different from all the rest
Louder and more shrill, a good sound of haunting
The voice of a Muslim caller at dawn
A bird, a Saturday, four directions and a need.
He sang this and did not sing
In that manner of speech afforded the heart:
That he was a man
Came to her not from any words, not like that
    But from the measure of his breathing
        From the five-ladder depth of his left eye
        The one that did not move, his one eye which
        While his right eye could move through the everyday
        Could only stay looking at her.
When she looked at this eye at first
The sight of it made a noise in her, a start,
A note somewhere at the top of the piano scales
Fear, almost; a grasped breath; a glass dropped.
In the moment was the music of being wanted.
    Or of wanting, but she could not think it.
Certainly she could only say no
The way anyone would after a glass falls
No and Jesus. And as an afterthought, that he should go away.
    Many years later she read a book and it took
    Her breath: how neatly the glasses for champagne
    Thrown by the fine heroes
    Broke against the walls holding fire.
    That this was a celebration.
    That this was the Continental, the European.
No, she said, to this thick railroad tie of a man

Who sang to her the oldest song, the one
Of being young, that he was a piccolo flute
In the small of her heart. *No*
She said, but said it with her mouth, not with her heart
Making no a spoken word, like all other words
So that he did not hear, so that he kept singing
Until one day it was enough, but not for her, not now:
Now, instead, the afternoon, which was kind
Which is what she was earlier, had only pretended for him
I am her, whispered it to him, let him be strong
In its arms one more time before it took him,
Holding tighter than a grandmother.
     This was not at all what he wanted
     But what he wanted he could not have.
     No, she said, and he could not get close enough
     Could not put the ear of his song heart
     Against her chest
     To know what the word meant, no.

3.
He had written no note for his daughter.
It had not been necessary.
She knew now what it would have been,
What the word *no* means
When it is pronounced, when the last half of it lingers, *o*
Imagined that the *o* was like this
     Together as if it were new nude in the afternoon
     They must have danced the wild Apache
     Without lunch, into the hours
     Imagining themselves French, striped shirt and berets
     Two carp on a rug in the ocean of the room
     Two June beetles, two bees
     Beings with impossible wings, pulleys from the roof

24

Pulling the two of them up like birthday piñatas
Two of them, then four: hands and legs
Tied more expertly than the best dream of an old salt sailor
Bread dough wound round and again into afternoon cakes,
Two, four, then six of them: all the parts of the face
Then twelve of them: their two faces together
Twenty-four then and thirty-six and words and breaths
Inside each other their tongues
Like the wings of hummingbirds in flight
Like bees, his fingers, faster than possible
That it was like this exactly.

4.
Her fame was as a maker of oval mats many years later
Mats for placement behind photographs,
How the old ones were, sometimes in colors
Sometimes to highlight, sometimes for support simply,
Always making the best faces.
But what she loved most, what was true for her
Was her firm putting of the tongues and most heavy parts
Of several men of the town, each on a different night
Sundays being specially reserved for the troubled boy
On a rancho several kilometers out of town,
Putting them slowly into her mouth, this best of all
And sucking there at them better
Than if she were drawing out the juice of an orange
Small hole made in it, the way children do
Squeezing out the everything.
It was, better described, this *deliverance* of her men
This taking out from their baby-arms
What it was that troubled them
So much all at once, so much like the stories
She had heard of the ghost being delivered,

25

Being let go, from the mouth
Exactly at the point of death.
She would trade nothing for this
For being able to say yes where others had said no.
To say yes, and watch her men die.
Die and then be brought back, to be strong at this
This was her power, this is what made her laugh
Being her mother and her father both
Being happy for them all
Never once making love to a man.

Two

The Scent of Unbought Flowers

After all, a man has a soul.
It is everything he has thought
and kept unspoken, each thing
he has felt and for which he could
find no reasonable name, no sound.
Because it can
his soul forgets the sky
and each time for a purpose
does the work of reinventing it.
Another man's soul has other
names for the constellations,
La Casserole for the Big Dipper,
other names for the failures
of rain,
other names for other names.
But each understands at the bottom
of itself, underneath even color,
under red, inside tin, and brick,
here perfectly each soul
understands the tiny machinery
of lizards,
their thousand beads and the place
of the *ay! Lázaro!* birds
when they call.
Understands heaven is the hottest
place, sweating on the top
of a woman, or underneath her
where the scent of unbought
flowers is,
knows that its power is like hands
connected without arms

to thin shoulders, but hands
nonetheless—that much strength
only, in a soul.
In a soul, where leaves do not
turn color to color—
that is the job of eyes
and of hunger—
nothing is so comfortable,
nothing in a soul is a padded
and fat chair.
A soul is that which has kissed
the shadowed edges
of overweight women in the night,
cuckooed as a bird out of a clock,
tiny, into their secret folds
and back,
finished with them.

The Queer Statue of Don Miguel

She had been in his hands.
This gave him the illusion of intimacy.
But the truth of this tangled communion,
this jungle they had made of themselves,
this putting of his soul between his teeth,
this Rousseau canvas of the tigers:
the effect on her, the truth for her of their enveloping,
the simpler truth, which she told him afterward:
> that it was not true, her kiss
> her polishings of his back
> or the falling of her thin skirts:
these newborn, second, and stronger words
gave him the despair of the impassioned
the despair redder than nasturtiums,
the nasturtiums which came out crimson that year;
these newwalking words gave him the knotted brow and raging
which pushed him under the high heel of the night
to the place where night pushes hardest down.
There he could move no longer.

And no, and no he dared not speak
though he felt himself a cage to thunder
for God might truly strike her down—
these would have been his instructional prayers
and even God would have listened to despair like his
so that even in his pains he took care to protect her.
But the sight of her full skirts
as they swept the narrow streets,
her skirts, would not leave him,
the sound of the full skirts of her voice
as it called to him, *Miguelín,* in a gentler night,

31

the full skirts of her arms as they had held him.
But as he had taken wildly the skirts down from her
now they were taken from him
it was not true, her kiss
her polishings of his back.
He paused in disgust at his lack of ease
a man tired of souls.

The year the nasturtiums came out crimson
Madeleine loved everyone within range.
Her skirts fell for each man
until the story of her newness,
the story of her half-moon breasts went dead.
She had left each one to his songs, and was gone
running next morning to the strong skins of another.
This one Miguelín—I point him out for you,
there, as I point him out for anyone who wishes
to see how he had gone searching for her
gone through the trail of houses to the room
where the oldest Martinez boy lived, to the back
bedroom of the store his brother Julio owned,
the store where Miguelín himself had bought string.
He stopped finally in this corner of the park
       her polishings of his back
where he hoped to see her walking the distance
between one man and another, hoped to hold her by the elbow
walk with her, say that he would wait for her
his Madeleine of the one night different
from the darknesses of other nights,
the darkest black stripe of the canvas tiger.
I point him out for you, there,
how he became stone in the waiting.

Snow Cones from the Old Carnivals

The scenery for eyes he'd seen with eyes,
  como los nogales ya crecidos,
the smell of smells, the press of Oaxacan jazz

with nose, with ears; he'd eaten flavored snow,
  antes, los raspados eran fuertes,
had put it in his mouth and sprayed that gold

all ice all over everything, the dress
  mango, platano, ciruela, coco,
it was his mother's best. But hulls of ice

were now like skins that animals have known,
  pero ya me siento bien cansado,
banana skins of snakes, their juices gone

like his, like eating colors, sucking blues
  lengua torpe, ojos ya nublosos.
to gray and then to nothing, getting old.

These nights had come, when color wasn't loud.
  Edad tiene el sabor de latas.
The ice now turned a black inside his mouth,

just cold, just night, in which some crowbirds sat
  "¡Come ya!" Soy viejo, y me hacen.
and he could see them seeing him, could taste

the flavor of their stares, their wanting him.
  ¡Vengan pajaros! Les doy mis ojos.
He'd spit it out again and then again,

but this one night he tongued those pepper crows,
  Son azules. Hasta un animal
and ate the ice that was their eyes: they'd know

the dark inside him, and he began to crawl.
  debe probar el sabor de algo.

Anciano en el porche del hospital

No sabes bastante para morir,
divirtiéndote con un matamoscas,
golpeando tus dedos, pies subidos,
desnudos, empujando la orilla
de la mesa grande y descolorida
como si la mesa fuera mujer.
Tú, portándote primero como un coronel
joven, látigo mocho en tus manos
como si tu fuerza única
venía de ese palo
como el bastón que detenía Moisés,
y entonces, enfadado de eso,
marcando el compás, disfrutándote
como si ese bastón fuera extensión
de tu sonrisa simple,
director de tu vida encanecida,
animando primero prontitud
y entonces torpeza,
Ni por un momento deseando perfección.
Tú, ¿quién eres que no te preocupas,
que nada más sigues
hora tras hora, verano tras verano
como si fueras animal
con solamente ruidos salvajes a dentro,
conociendo nada de la muerte,
durmiendo a través del invierno?
Cuando te pregunto, como siempre,
en voz baja para no estorbar
alguna cosa dolorosa a dentro,
me das solamente tus ojos,
como dos palabras extrañas

en medio de un libro,
pronunciadas sin sentido, vacías,
como un vaso hermoso es vacío.

Old Man on the Hospital Porch

You don't know enough to die,
amusing yourself with a flyswatter,
hitting your toes, feet raised,
naked, pushing the side
of the big and colorless table
as if that table were a woman.
You, acting first like a young
colonel, small whip in your hands
as if your only strength
came from that stick
like the staff that Moses held,
and then, tired of that,
keeping time, enjoying yourself
as if that baton were the extension
of your simple smile,
conductor of your gray life,
encouraging first quickness
and then heaviness,
not for one moment desiring perfection.
You, who are you that you do not worry,
who only carries on
hour after hour, summer after summer
as if you were an animal
with only wild noises inside,
knowing nothing of death,
sleeping through the winter.
When I ask you, like always,
in a low voice so as not to disturb
some painful thing inside,
you give me only your eyes,
like two strange words

37

in the middle of a book,
pronounced without meaning, empty,
like a pretty glass is empty.

The Famous Boxer Reies Madero Lives

The man whose name was strongest
here now. Imagine that.
The fact of it is almost too much to fit
into our small heads.

But, he says, now he must limp
and hold his hand tight
on the head of a gargoyle cane.

None here will be fooled so easily.
He was the one who killed two men in the ring,
the old kind of ring that was dirty
with sweat and canvas and fingers.
So it is agreed: no one will come near him
even still, he has been too strong,
too loud and too admired.
Some things must not change.

But, he says, he can kill no longer.
He has tried, and failed.
There is no cause to run,
his cousin from the south the lowland Chiapas
can be written to, and asked.
In another town he had grown so angry,
but he could not keep it,
the anger had fallen from him as a tooth.

No one believes him.
Each has said to himself
my own eyes have lied to me
and have worked with my ears.
Evil here is at work in the body
of a crooked man, whose crooked mouth
will not speak for its honest self.
The famous boxer Reies Madero has been
even more powerful than that
which tricks us now.

The Seeds That Come Through the Air

After a particular hour in the night,
maybe three, a farm ceases to exist.
The work of a corn root
and the thinnest dream of a calloused man
are pure then, and no Englishman's word
attends honestly to what they do precisely
now, together at a fat and bursting moment
that does not exist, which is to say at best,
cannot be explained, even at that moment.
Pressed at this hour together they are
the thousand different things, the remembered
face, misplaced objects, the sexual dreams,
amputated arms and the eyes of goats, yellow eyes,
hunger, each thing at that moment, inside the night
of these two, moving light-legged
from man to root in the purest black, black
which is the secret gift of levitation,
distilled night, things indistinguishable, invisible
as all the shadows that a person walking sees
clinging about, parked in the fragile daytime,
collected now all together, edge held to edge,
ganged up into a single face, a single barrel-point.
We have spent our lives lighting up the night,
and failed. An indiscriminate bird moves.
A corn root and a thin dream
touch then, more discreetly, more carefully
than two Brazilian lovers might, and go on.

Chileño Boys

The Chileño boys pull their fish by the fins in the dirt
and sing
about the old times and the women they will know, Mariquita
and Caras,
the girls in the dreams of—the when they will be men.
Fish, they sell
what they can, what is caught, what they hold in their arms
for the day.
The Chileño boys pull their feet by the strings through the dirt
and sing
confusing themselves in the inside jungle with sons and fathers,
themselves lost
halfway out into the years that have been and will be,
long,
not different, not different, they say, not different from you.

Watching a Face Go Away

That farmer blue, that man without money
who so must settle for this, that poor man's blue,
that tin with flecks everything was made of:
next to the basin whose color was pitted sky
he found the cup full of caked salt.
He broke some of it into gravel bits
licked a finger as he would to find wind
and got enough parts of the salt to stick
so he could brush his teeth, but too hard,
and he knew it; after the gritting he caught
his tongue between his index finger and thumb
pulling off the taste of night
persimmon from the hours of lying.
This picture of himself pulling off his tongue
drew him in the small mirror to his eyes
where night, too, had formed
at the lashes and the edges of the white.
Last night had wanted him. Like the salt
it had tried to harden him.
But this morning of a Thursday he takes
from his eye the pieces of himself
the pieces of what the night had almost won
of what has leaked, of what has listened
and cannot be forced back, takes them,
drops these pieces of his face to the ground.

Island of the Three Marias

The pale nuns of St. Joseph are here
in groups, on the island of the just
arrived from having been somewhere else
and will be leaving soon without scars.

There are really four islands here
but the others are simply ignored.
No one has thought to ask why,
not Faustino, his wife, the children
the others, or even these white nuns
not in a Christian place, prison islands
inherited from the lepers who decomposed.
On this particular island the family makes
a living, and this is their punishment.
A burden placed in the hands of Faustino
the poor man who kills.

This place is the physical moment
for which the nuns are Easter lilies.
White is the frayed habits of the young
women who will not be women here.

He is too young, never married
who feels the two pains:
north, he could have no woman,
here he could, and had none.
He erased the laughing, his own
laughing that echoed—he said came—
from the mouths of those around him
with the needle in his leg
sometimes even through his pants

when he felt that way he felt,
crying pain he called *wife*.
Because of his soft noises, then
he sometimes was loaned Mrs. Marez,
Faustino let him, thank you Faustino,
and when she left, whore! to Mrs. Marez.
He knew the truth which was dreaming
to leave this place to do again
what made his father proud
who, carefully, had shown him how.

White is the coldest color handed down
from old to new like one photograph,
like the story of the child martyrs
or the stale candies said to be blessed.

The man in the suit did not care.
His wife who did not come here
suffered from the embarrassment
of marriage with the one
too formal for this frivolous place
because he could be nothing else,
too important to have liked his name,
to have liked the boys
who were everywhere smiling at him.
Fresco Peach, the name he invented.
It reminded him of something
American western, Frisco Pete,
something tough but not quite
and that is better. He stayed inside
so no one would laugh here, and never
told his name to a woman.
A man is ugly, he says to himself,
a man then suddenly stops running.

A Man Walks as if Trapped

No hunter can catch him
lithe and properly built
hatless like a steep hill.
His test of youth is this:
not to wish forgotten
the fifth stake, once
building a fence.
That he can resist
the blowing hair
of a nice daughter
is simple enough
midwinter, one night.
He is an enemy
to the lions
a good painter
many women hiding
what he is.

As though we allow it
neither of them says anything.
There are moments
suspended in flocks
of sparrows left blooming
never seen by two people,
moments the housemaid rapidly
offers apologetic noises.
A standing conversation, then
they are.
Such intimacy
there is only one
movement feeling

only her own body
feeling her deciding
I might as well work slowly,
here is a man.

A Man Then Suddenly Stops Moving

The old Russian spits up a plum
fruit of the rasping sound
he has stored in his throat
all these lonely years

made in fact lonely by his wife
who left him, God knows
without knowing how to cook for himself.

He examines the plum
notes its purplish consistency
almost the color and shape of her buttocks
whose circulation was bad

which is why he himself wears a beret:
black, good wool, certainly warm enough
the times he remembers.

He shoots the plum
to the ground like a child
whose confidence is a game of marbles

whose flick of a thumb
is a smile inside his mouth
knowing what he knows will happen.

But his wife, Marthe
does not spill out
when the plum breaks open.

Instead, it is a younger self
alive and waving
just the size he remembers
himself to have been.

The old Russian puts him onto his finger
like a parakeet
and sits him on the shelf
with the pictures.

For the rest of his days
he nags himself constantly
into a half-sleep
surprised by this turn of events.

The Carlos Who Died, and Left Only This

If an eye could be a whip
his would be,
the sort of whip that the wind
sometimes is
slamming absolutely shut
a door
at a moment he could not anticipate
or want
and his brows are the sky,
latches
that sometimes slip to allow
this wind,
whip, like the lips of a single mouth
sometimes opened where no opening seemed to be
allowing a tongue so improbably
to kiss
a girl on the edge of a falling chair
and if hands could be anything
these too would be
what they are
now, a corral, an orchard,
nine thick spoons
lying folded on the clean chest
of a borrowed suit
that was returned.

On January 5, 1984, El Santo the Wrestler Died, Possibly

The thing was, he could never be trusted.
He wore the silver mask even when he slept.
At his funeral as reported by all the Mexican news services
The pall bearers also put on their faces
Sequined masks to honor him, or so it was said.
The men in truth wore masks as much to hide from him
That he would not see who was putting him into the ground
And so get angry, get up, and come back after them
That way for which he was famous.
His partner el atomico pretended to think
There was no funeral at all.
He would have had to help el santo be angry
Come like the Samson running against the pillars
These men were, holding up the box
In which el santo was trapped;
Would have had to angle his head down, come at them
Mount them three men to a shoulder
As he ran through the middle, ducking under the casket
Bowling them down like all the other times
Giving el santo just a moment to breathe, get strong.

He will be missed
But one must say this in a whisper, and quickly.
One knows of the dead, of their polite habit of listening
Too much, believing what they hear, and then of their caring.
One knows of the dead, how it all builds up
So that finally something must be said.
One knows of the year in which the town of Guaymas
Had its first demonstration of a tape recorder.
It confirmed only what was already known:

That people speak. And that the voice of the wind
Captured finally, played back slowly
Given its moment to say something of lasting importance
Made only a complaint.
If el santo were to hear of his being missed
He might get hold of the wind, this voice of the dead,
And say too much, the way the best wrestlers do
With all the yelling.
So one will always be responsible enough only to whisper
The best things about el santo
Out of concern for the crops and the sapling trees.
This much was decided at the funeral.

The decision to whisper was not too much.
One had to be suspicious of this man with a mask
Even as he reached out to shake your hand,
That you might be flung and bent around
Knocked on the head and forced to say
How glad you are to meet him, and his uncle;
How suspicious that hand, which he always raised
More slowly than a weightlifter's last possible push
As if he too were suspicious of you
That you might at the last second
Be the Blue Demon after all—*el demonio azul: ¡aha!*
        he recognizes you, *¡but too late!* that you might
In this last moment avoid his hand raised to shake
Hook the crook of your arm into his
And flip him with a slam to a cement canvas.
No, he could not be trusted
And he could not trust you.

In his last years very far from 1942
The year he gave his first bruise to another man
One received as a greeting no hand from him any longer.

A raised eyebrow, perhaps, *good morning to you,*
Just visible through the mask on his morning walk.
This was his greeting, one man to another, now.
But even then he could not be trusted
Had not slipped with age even an inch:
As he moved the hairy arm of his brow up and down
Like a villain taking possession of the widow's house,
If one quickly did not get out of his way—
Well, then, he kept it moving up and down, had gotten you
Had made you imagine his eyebrow
Making the sound of a referee's hand
Slam beating the canvas ten times
Telling you that you have lost.

The Lesson of Walls

Florencio built a wall and told no one why.
He was stubborn this way about things.
Too beautiful to be described by the ill-educated
tax assessor in this small but honorable town,
it was entered in no book and so did not exist
in that way that other walls are known.
Florencio stood behind his invisible wall
and so quite reasonably was invisible himself
and could do for the first time whatever he chose.
People came from the big cities on Sunday noons
to see this thing that did not by its nature exist
and Florencio, Florencio as he had always wanted
since the early days of his troublesome schooling,
made his five ugly faces at the faces of the people,
inverting his eyelids and pushing to the side his nose
so as to look like the devil that children imagine,
and he made sounds with his mouth to his pleasure.
But through the years finally he grew
bored of his invisible fame, and his mouth, or entirely
his face, became tired, so that it rested,
let its weight fall, and it rolled over onto itself
in its leisure making Florencio wrinkled and heavy.
One morning he took a workman's hammer to his wall.
People saw him again, and he found himself
drawing up his face, as one might pull up
a stomach in front of a favorite aunt.
He was young again, and unhappy, and happy.
This business of the invisible,

54

of a thing too beautiful for the weak
recreations of words and of penmanship,
had taught Florencio who was a young fine horse of a boy
again, why a man builds a common wall
ugly, two bricks uneven, why he lets the paint chip.

Panfilo's Birthday

In October on the afternoon
of his fourth birthday
Panfilo told his father
the things he had learned.
The leaves have changed.
They look now like the paper
trash in Portillo's paint store.
No, said his father, after all,
today was not his birthday.
Leaves were the colors of flame
like the picnic fires they made
on the banks of Sonoita Creek.
He told him to come back tomorrow.

The air is too cold, Panfilo said.
It feels like the insides of
the freezer where the chickens are kept.
No, the air is warm, his father said,
like the way the ice burns when touched
as it freezes over the shallow parts
of the creek on some nights.
Neither was today his birthday, he said,
come back again tomorrow.

I don't know what you want, said Panfilo.
Is it that nothing here smells
like the wet sand and rocks of the creek?
His father nodded his head
from side to side
and Panfilo left without aging.

The next day Panfilo came again,
but this time he said nothing at all.
His father stood, and nodded up
then down, and said that it was true,
today he was four, but not older.
Of that he should take advantage.

Nicanor, Saturday

Where is it that a man can find no reason to weep in secret, in secret because he is ashamed to weep from pain, ashamed because he can recall no mention of other men weeping, no mention of his father or his grandfather ever weeping? It is not here. And it is not anywhere else that any of the neighbors he thought of had been, they had been only here. But only here was not the only place. The Incredible Mr. Balance had said so and who could not believe such a man, such a man among men—a man among children. Children, thought Nicanor, nothing more for he was one of these men and he should know. What Nicanor knew was that he wept, openly but in that secret way of his that was only his because his shame had made it his. Nicanor laughed.

And laughed and laughed at all the things the Incredible Mr. Balance could do, and laughed at all the things he talked about, things he said were not magic at all, not even special or hard to get and own, and the can-opener that was electric and had a knife sharpener in back? Well, that was one of the easiest. But not here. And women anyone can have, if you've got money, and sometimes, even if you don't. Women, and nobody knows. Nobody cares, nobody but you. You.

"Who are you, Incredible Mr. Balance?"

"Here I am God. I am God today."

Nicanor stared at God.

"Tomorrow I may change my mind. I may change my mind because you have changed your mind."

"Can God change His mind? Can God not be God?"

"Yes. Yesterday I was not God, and tomorrow I will not be God. You can be God tomorrow."

"No, tomorrow I cannot. Tomorrow I must work, to-morrow I will yell when I come home, tomorrow I might cut these fingers picking the prickly pears off the cactus for dinner. Tomorrow my skin sweats."

"Here, lick my skin."

Nicanor licked His skin and shrugged his shoulders.

"I am the taste of all things."

The taste of the Incredible Mr. Balance was salty, good on food but not off the skin, good and not good, but salt and nothing else. The taste was gone and nothing else filled his mouth. Nicanor closed his mouth and walked away. He walked until his throat, his mouth chuckled, until his mouth became full of the laughing that now he did not want to understand, full of the laughing that made tears fall down the back of his throat because he could let no one else see them in his eyes, tears that made his mouth salty. Nicanor tried to pull the tears out of his mouth with his hands, his fingers, but they, too, were salty, his hands and his fingers were pure salt, more than his tears, but no, that couldn't be. Nicanor could not be God, he could not, he had no time, he had no skills, no balance, no magic.

No, he laughed, no, God must be God, he cried then, please, God must be God, and tomorrow, tomorrow especially, tomorrow is Sunday.

Three

The Inquietude of a Particular Matter

Ventura had hair of the jungle
long like the gatling words
of the monkeys and the parrots
like the vines and roots without end
all pulled back knotted and tight
with the help, the insistence
of her mother who had cheeks
like persimmons, her face
always tasting their peel,
her mother using the energy
of that taste to pull
so that the face part
of Ventura's young girl head
became skull, white bone
and sockets, big clack teeth
like in the cartoon, unconnected,
almost, clack clacking so
she could not help
sounding like the fat ducks
that every day she fed
after she stopped her work
in the peeling secretariat
of a third but ambitious
supervisor to the federal railroads,
fed the ducks every day popcorn,
palomitas, and the one day
she could not because of the snow,
snow for the first time
she could remember this early,
this far to the south,
the ducks opened their mouths anyway

and ate the snow, the white bits
they thought had come from her.
She laughed and opened
her mouth, also, making a sound
in that late afternoon
so sacred in its one freedom
that the crickets stopped to listen
but no less than he.

Clemente had watched her
from behind the bougainvilleas,
had smoked his colored cigarette
watching her in this moment
then letting her go, simply,
like smoke to its most secret place,
to the place smoke always goes,
this Ventura leaving a memory
sweet like cane in his eyes
so that the rest of his body
caught fire with jealousy.
The world had always erupted
through him, always bad,
but not this time: this time
he wished to whisper the Spanish
love words he had dreamed,
how long they were, he wished
to let these words kick
their fine heels through the fat
wall of freedoms
breaking through to the side
of what might be
but he dared not.
In this town, he knew well,
in this life, one must wait.

Nothing could be more simple.
He blew circles of new smoke
the size of himself standing,
the large himself
where the pain most certainly was,
wishing he could so easily
erase the pain with his hands,
put his hands fisted
into the face of a bad man
but he could not.
The inquietude of this matter
of love, of loving how she saw
the ducks, how she laughed out
her true self in that moment,
how he wanted her
he could not endure.
But he would. This was his test,
to say nothing.

How a Circus Works

Twinkling in that way they say
when she performed her wild secret,
the eyes of Mariette were fired and moving
as if she kept them barely happy in her face,
tied barely like stallions or big Shepherd dogs
and if she would dare to let go
even for a moment, if the thin rein should break
they would run out from their place
out over to the fine grass of the distance,
turn over and rub their backbones
along the ground and move and move
maybe not ever coming back, not ever.

He was one juggler in the third ring
of this minor entertainment, *El Circo Magnífico*
fresh from the inhuman jungles of Chiapas,
but he also had eyes, this particular Florencio.
He tried like the colored balls to balance
his eyes, yes! but was not fast enough here,
so that his eyes could not help but fall,
always one a little more than the other
into the folded recesses of extra face
that he had built up through the thin years,
one eye heavier with the weight of things
carried in his life, with work, with his mother
who had died, with his sisters who went hungry,
one eye lower, less visible, this was the eye
most talked about, this eye was the one
weighted also with the pounds of dream
she, Mariette, made him carry.

This she of the wild secret married him
because of that eye, how it held
the room of a steamship trunk all for her
with its border marks and Eiffel Tower stamp.
Not one in the circus understood exactly
how Mariette and this Florencio could not look
straight at each other, could not bear it.
But she was too beautiful, he would say,
too full of plums, of peacock feathers,
and he was sure that some day, any minute,
she would leave him at a gallop, that quickly,
so he would not, dared not, look up with his eyes,
his eye, with which he would only be too slow.

He would simply just not leave, that Florencio,
she would say, that old fig cake,
that torn doily, she could not get rid of him,
and even when she and her juggler,
of whom she was ashamed, needed to talk, or see
each other, they did not like you and I
look up, not like that, nothing so easy.
He saw her instead most safely
with his second heart, with the thousand
large eyes of a heart that lived
in his fingers when they touched her,
in his strong walking legs, in the strong
shoulder of his careful words
which could not say anything tender,
this she did not allow, not once.
And she, this wild Mariette, saw Florencio only
in her dreams, on the fine grass
of the distance where the Shepherd dogs,
the stallions that were her sad eyes,
ran to him like animals, and he took them.

The Job of a Shirt

In the Brown Street orchards a humped-back man can get a job
there, out of sight, the orange tree leaves
will hide him and the fruit, about the fruit,
no one will ever know who has touched it, and they will put it
in their mouths without a sound, pass it over their lips.
He is a strong man in the fields, a man simply, most anciently.
In an orchard a man understands strength, measures it
in bushels held on an arm, sweat staining the chest of a shirt.
But for the humped-back man a shirt is not
a shirt, cannot do what a shirt must, cover
him, cover the pain from which this new body has come:
this hump was once a woman, was still a woman, who thought

his hands are the rain, smooth
on my back, a second spine
curved perfectly with mine,
that strong, that familiar,
I like it. It is not always
good, but I like it, yes.
If it is strong enough, this
second spine, these hands,
I will give them food,
something to hold, to take
from me. If they stay strong.
Only if they stay strong.

A Short History of Guaymas

The true history of the town of Guaymas is a sham as if
the histories of towns could be true,
truer than the things we say to each other
to get each other's clothes off now and fast.
The true history of Guaymas is told in eight separate volumes
the same thing in each, eight versions of nothing
more than what never has existed, there was
no general who did *that,* not ever, not anywhere.
Someone told the story to impress his Mariquita
and it worked God it worked, so it had to be real,
it was the thing that got her clothes to come off,
this story of the dashing general with thin moustaches
and a cape who with his single arm sang
the difficult song of violence louder than the rest
but on the right side of things
and it was this business of saving the six sisters of mercy
against which this Catholic Mariquita could not win,
could only melt like sugars into the arm
of this one particular history, the one that must be true
even for hard Catholic girls from the desert north,
melt like sugars into the arm, into the face of a man
who talked through the seasons and the seasons of the night.

The Man Who Called His Wife

He had given her from out of his mouth,
or farther, from out of the dark and red
a private and small kiss
and it was a real thing like a spoon
or a boot, an object, for the first time
in their lives, and she took it
not with her cheek or her pressed lips
but with her hand, and she held it
there, first for hours, turning it,
rolling it more firmly than a rosary,
then put it away in the carved box
with the herbs, the true wild lilac
and the orange blossoms collected
through all the slow years of her life,
an herb taken from this valley,
a blossom from that.
A kiss in a box becomes a sharp thing,
though, and one fast day with it,
one speeded hour she opened up
her ankles without pain, without change
in her tight face which was not for her
a real face any longer.
This was his plan, and he called her
now, and she opened them to let out
the heavy blood, that way making herself
lighter, able to dance again, lightly,
the *cumbias* and the red dress dances
the way her Florencio first had liked
her, more lightly than ever before
ever by anyone, up in the strong air,
floating easily, and smiling, smiling,

laughing because she hears him say
the stars have pearled your neck,
they have confused their place
and they come to be with you, laughing
she flicks those light ankles back
and forth like the ballet dancers
she had seen at the roofless theater
in Guaymas, fast like the machine guns
at the movies in Nogales, bees' wings
back and forth, so and again, then
she jumps up, jumps up and down
using only the strength of her ankles,
like ballerinas, handsome ankles,
in the large and beautiful mirror,
up and down until she cannot.

The Mouths of Two People

She threw her Paraguayan blanket down
on a section of the shore's grasses
and at first perfectly we sat there
in that peculiar kind of wildest comfort,
talking with our mouths in between figs
about what mouths discuss: the sky,
the thumbflick scattered and jagged minnows,
the unkind heat out there beyond the cottonwoods,
but the real heat, the hot of the night
that finds its way into the body
which cannot then be still, be shushed,
this is what our second mouths asked about,
the mouths that are where eyes appear to be,
mouths whose secret lips are subtle lids,
whose words like the wind are barely heard,
these mouths ask about each other's skin,
about what our feet might look like, feel like,
held by the water instead of our shoes,
ask about what holding each other's calves
might feel like, there among the spring reeds
among the figs and the white chocolate
spread over the blanket on which I have eaten
her hair and all the notable parts of her body,
turning back the corduroy and useless cotton,
the zippers and her snaps most singularly placed.
I watch her, too, fill on my hands,
fill on the shape of my legs to the hip,
fill on the curved part of the letter p
that is the top part of a young man's leg.
Wandering on the blanket in the grasses and reeds
we fill each other with our picnic,

tell spiraling lies to make us stay, and stay,
our true mouths saying to each other
how we long to lie together,
to become recognizable fixtures of the sky,
some Orion at which others might easily point
saying how slowly the constellation moves,
how the stars in its skin seem to fit.

Four

The Handsome Bougainvilleas of the Garden

I have heard a story.
When my grandmother was a small woman
the town in which she lived was made of people
who used their own feet as shoes,
feet grown hard, so much leather
I see it even today after so many years
so like the skins of the leather animals,
the cows, and the lizards.
As night came they stood around themselves
waiting, but impatiently, as if at the line
ready just before the race
at the Elks Club picnic, she says, just
like that, like how your uncle can't wait.
And when the food came, the beans and the cane
leftovers of the big house food,
they let themselves eat it
abandoning themselves to an arithmetic,
an algebra, a visible reduction
to basic equations, to high school biology:
eat something, be a little less hungry.
Tears came not from hunger, but from eating,
from knowing it would not work,
from the sorrow knowledge brings.
Having known hunger for corn the way they had
hunger for coffee so intimately
so much as a handsome lover
but a lover who is cruel, without callouses,
so like a man who takes his cane to a wife,
they knew they could never be full,
never be not hungry, never without room.
Still they ate until sickness came

if there was enough,
and kept eating the fresh memory of dinner
even after that, even if it had come back up
in the sure manner of those caned wives
who will not leave their unshaven husbands
because at least they know there will be no
shaving, and what is out in the garden
full of bougainvilleas, or in a suit
Sunday on a walk and smiling
they do not know. My grandmother
shakes her head. I try not to look at her feet.
It would be worse.
They had heard stories.

How the Mouth Works

1
A sound, laughter
fell from her mouth
out carelessly
in the manner of those
women who have lived
longest, who have been
forever our aunts,
fell as a liquid
goatmilk still warm
onto her pale blouse
then skirt,
which was long,
and so it went
but without wetness
without the dark
marks of rain
down to the floor
over to its particular
corner, staying there,
seeping into the wood,
almost always too quiet
but for the *moments*
when it was not,
and each time someone
suggests as someone
must always do
that this room is not
truly hers,
not her, that the walls
are not her skin,

that the laughter
at such a *moment* in the room
is a squeaking board
come loose, or somesuch idea—
when this is said at last
laughter comes, then,
from our mouths, which work
this way, this laughter
unmistakable, having come
up from where we have stepped
in this tired room,
from the particular place
in the corner of the floor,
laughter
which has come up the legs
of these blue pants,
up the shirt and higher,
this laugh
which is hers
as much as our eyes are,
then—this is the *moment*—
having moved up
into the mouth
my mouth this time,
she does laugh, yes.
We can hear it,
hear that it is long
and for nothing funny.

2
Her dream in the sheets
of the night drawn up
right next to her face,

next to where she breathed,
had been recurring.
It came like blood,
always the same, always
about the first time
she had seen a ball
for bowling, that game
where all the men were
for all those years,
and how the ball was held
precisely, and this was
what her dream was,
how this ball was held
just so, with the three
fingers inserted,
but rather into the head
of a large halfblack cat,
her second Miguelito,
the one that ran away.
Into his two eyes
and his sad mouth.
This was her one dream
and in it, then, she
became the cat.
This was why her mouth
was falling and sad
on these last mornings,
two fingers of a bad dream
going into her, but upside down
so she could see,
two fingers going into
her, instead of babies
coming out, and the third
into her stomach

pushing out the breath.
That is how her navel
must have gotten there,
someone in the night
as she was asleep
and too young to speak
must have done this,
and in her dream
these were her scars,
made bigger again, and
again, three fingers
into them, her first
Miguelito, his fingers,
the man who ran away.

3
And then one morning
as I slept in her bed
to comfort her, her
baby that never came,
she sat up like an L
and I saw her, saw
that the dream this time
had not ended.
She spoke to me
in the words of her dream,
so that the words
of this world
must have gone
with her. To help her.
Our names, the names of salt
and *chile*, salt
y las papas

cociendo en la mañana.
She spoke, and I held
her new word in my hands,
held the moan
to comfort it,
I held it in both hands
because I had to.
The sound of this thing
I had watched,
how it pulled out, long,
as if her tongue
all the while
all the years I had seen her,
had been the plain
and thin head
of a fisherman's eel
finding its chance now
to go, get out, but slow
in the only way
it could move
through a small mouth
after so much waiting.
I held it, this word,
held it across
the palms of my two hands
and it was longer
than any man's arm.

Combing My Hair in the Hall

Each time the doors to her room were opened
a little of the gathered light left
and the small room became blacker
moving somewhere in a twilight toward night.
And then a little of the light left
not her room, but her falling face
as each time she opened the smaller doors
that were her wooden eyes.
She talked only with her mouth then
no longer with the force of her wild eyes
and that, too, made her less,
each word leaving her now
as the way her firm bones had abandoned her.
Then she spoke with her woman's hands
only, no words left, then only with her smell
which once had been warm, *tortillitas,*
or like sugar breads just made.
In the half-words of our other language,
in the language of the new world
of which she had had time to show me
only half, I tried to speak to her,
to fill her up, to tell her the jokes
of the day, and fill her too much
with laughing, fill her fat like she had been,
and my brother Tomás tried too, we
touched her, were made to touch her,
we kissed her even, lips trying
to quickly press back the something
as children even we could feel
but whose name she had not told us,
and as we kissed her, bent and kissed her,

we could smell her, I shivered, and we both
breathed out hard when we had to
put our lips there, like later we would learn
to drink *pulque* and be men, trying even that
to push her back into herself.
But she was impatient with us, or smarter,
or quicker, so that we did smell her,
she made us, and taste the insides of her,
and take her in small parts with us
but not like drink, not like men—instead,
like the smell of bread taken by the heart
into the next day, or into dreams.
Every night she wanted to be young again
as she slept there on her bed
and in the night, in the minute she could
no longer talk, and did not smell, or wake,
she was, again, young: we
opened our mouths
and asked words about her, cried
bits of ourselves out through our eyes,
each sigh expelled, each tear,
each word said now making us,
us less, not her, each word gone
making room in ourselves for her,
so that one day, again, she laughs hard,
a Thursday, four voices stronger, five,
laughs at something none of us understands,
standing there, comb in hand, laughs
at something silly, or vain, or the story
of the six sisters of mercy, perhaps, she
just laughs looking at all of her new faces
full in the mirror at the end of the hall.

Kicking the Slowest Boy

His breath smelled when he spoke
because his insides were rotting.
As a child he had eaten dirt
and his mother had said all right.
He eats it, she would say,
because there is something there
that he needs.
He grew, but not much
and his mornings became apples
and black coffee out of one cup.
His secret was that the apples
from the orchards grew
from trees, and trees grew in dirt.
With each apple he swallowed
his insides chased each other,
the little chases of children,
quick, out of breath, the chases
of boys playing tag, back
and forth and back without plan,
boys running and falling,
kicking the slowest, too many times
laughing, and then too hard
like a father who has worked
since birth and then one day
must punish his son, but goes too far,
so the boy starts to cry,
to feel pain, and they, too,
can feel it, these tag boys,
these insides of the man, aching,
yet they will not stop,
even out of breath, Ricardo,

Pachi, Julio, Rubén and every one,
the boys he remembers, the boy
he was, who fell to the ground
and held onto it as they kicked him,
held it like later he would hold
a woman, too long, too desperately—
himself young and all of them
running so fast still, but now
out of him, out of his old mouth,
each one yelling with the pain
memory brings, into the sink.
I would watch this man
who had the face of my uncle
come out of the bathroom on these days.
These were his insides he left
and he was glad to trade them,
to trade these pieces of what he was
in exchange for the power to eat
another apple, to build himself again
from the beginning with new pieces
of earth, to hold the earth near him
as apples, but these were the green,
wild apples that made the pain
that was his woman inside.
But that was what his woman was
he told me every morning,
so I dream of him happy now
in the woman arms of the ground.

Pirrincito's Word

No one dared make a sound
in the days when Latin was spoken
when dresses and veils and fine ties were worn
so that by accident he was given birth
in a corner of the Catholics' church
where his mother did not scream, or speak.
And he, when he breathed, he only breathed,
making no birthing sound, no cry
and the people were open-mouthed who saw this,
firmly reassured at that moment of their silence
which they have kept in every church
even after the changes, the loud songs and guitars
and the beards and the wafer they will not touch.

The boy grew until he was fourteen
and a word caught hard like a fishhook
in his throat, and that word was all
he could say, and then all he could think.
He turned it over in his mouth like a hard candy
and it gave him the quick and clean breaths
of the young blue and white parochial girls.
Because he repeated it, he understood the word
intimately like a ridge in the mouth
or a particular brown mark on the body,
and in his life this word became his job,
from which he drew his only pleasure.

In these later years the people who had witnessed
his birth, or those who had heard of it—
it is the silent things people talk about—
these people who saw him now with the word stuck

felt that this was a sign visited upon them
especially, a warning plainly that even without
a priest they understood, and took to heart.

The truth of it was
that his letters were still letters,
thoughts still thoughts.
He was not crazy, or taken, only
writing letters to the Chinese,
who gave importance
to such things as he dreamed.

Today the women come faithfully still,
black-headed, creased, and half-sized
after many years, always older and with a veil
elaborately constructed of foreiç laces
and with scapulars around their necks
and with worn hands.
They come early, and in pain, for Pirrincito.
It is not that someone has died.

I Would Visit Him in the Corner

He was the uncle who when he was young
and lying down had a spider crawl
into the large hole of his left ear and stay

through the night. Even after it was crushed
on the side of his head and he saw the legs
he never could believe it was gone

and so that ear was always stopped up
even though he would stand sometimes
like a swimmer jumping up and down

with his head cocked. It kept him from dying
in the war because they would not take him.
But he said he died anyway, and had nightmares

that crawled. And his ear grew bigger
because he kept hitting it, and when he was old
it became his habit, even when it bled.

Finally in the red night scratching
with no one to see and nothing to hold
the spider carelessly left him.

The Language of Great-Aunts

The great-aunts have a corner, and wrinkled skin
indistinguishable from their thick stockings,
and they invariably speak in the other language
of which we, as children, are able to recognize
only the commands, which are obvious, and the narrow
eyes, which make them law, drawn overly tight.

And their smiles are also long and tight,
black and without real teeth, scars on the skin
but only slight ones; red lips pressed, narrow,
their smiles are like the lines on their stockings,
which as two boys, at our height, we recognize
and wonder if these lines also speak some language.

And they do: theirs is the visible language
that when these women chew, only their mouths are tight
and immediately, because we are down there, we recognize
that, if they chewed harder, their wrinkled skin
would chew too, jiggling under their faces like the stockings
which are too big because their legs have grown too narrow.

But if we laugh, we get again the quick pin-narrow
eyes, who themselves speak a third language
more powerful than the line mouths of the stockings.
The eyes of the great-aunts disappear when drawn tight
and conspire somewhere under their spiderwebbed skin
made more webbed by attempts, not to warn, but to recognize.

We are never sure what exactly they are trying to recognize:
who we are, perhaps, or what we've done, and the narrow
amount of us they admit through the eyelids into that skin

is the part in us, inside, that makes us recognize
at these moments that our stomachs grow muscle-tight
and we change our big attentions fast from their stockings.

Because we are still too much children, their stockings
allow us to understand what others will not, to recognize
like commands what their eyes are really saying: how tight
their lives have grown, making their insides more narrow
than outside; words, black lines, eyes, all are one language,
saying *too tight now, too weak inside to hold up this skin.*

We watch their stockings grow larger, their legs more narrow.
We recognize by touch the verbs of this single language.
Later we stay tight, and pull in mirrors at our strong skin.

Dinner

As Tacaná erupted in the south
Mexican jungles, my father was born
and this is the sound he makes
when he eats, with his mouth,
with the way he breathes through his nose.
I am afraid of volcanoes,
I have seen the pictures, the way
they are shaped like the ant hills,
and he spits small seeds out.
I watch them crawl to the far corners
of the room, toward the spiders,
toward the spaces in the chipped wall.
I am the only one who can see,
the one who must take them in my hands,
never let go, juggle, balance, dance.
As Tacaná erupted in the south
birds came into my grandmother's house
and saved themselves up in the rafters,
where I was waiting for them.

Seniors

William cut a hole in his Levi's pocket
so he could flop himself out in class
behind the girls so the other guys
could see and shit what guts we all said.
All Konga wanted to do over and over
was the rubber band trick, but he showed
everyone how, so nobody wanted to see
anymore and one day he cried, just cried
until his parents took him away forever.
Maya had a Hotpoint refrigerator standing
in his living room, just for his family to show
anybody who came that they could afford it.

Me, I got a French kiss, finally, in the catholic
darkness, my tongue's farthest half vacationing
loudly in another mouth like a man in Bermudas,
and my body jumped against a flagstone wall,
I could feel it through her thin, almost
nonexistent body: I had, at that moment, that moment,
a hot girl on a summer night, the best of all
the things we tried to do. Well, she
let me kiss her, anyway, all over.

Or it was just a flagstone wall
with a flaw in the stone, an understanding cavity
for burning young men with smooth dreams—
the true circumstance is gone, the true
circumstances about us all then
are gone. But when I kissed her, all water,
she would close her eyes, and they into somewhere
would disappear. Whether she was there

or not, I remember her, clearly, and she moves
around the room, sometimes, until I sleep.

I have lain on the desert in watch
low in the back of a pick-up truck
for nothing in particular, for stars, for
the things behind stars, and nothing comes
more than the moment: always now, here in a truck,
the moment again to dream of making love and sweat,
this time to a woman, or even to all of them
in some allowable way, to those boys, then,
who couldn't cry, to the girls before they were
women, to friends, me on my back, the sky over me
pressing its simple weight into her body
on me, into the bodies of them all, on me.

A Man Keeps Strong

In a hospital bed
a man has no car, no tool
to show his worth.
Expertise around him
is a superhumanly taut
bottom sheet, white, cotton,
a clean under fingernails.
In this second world everyone
smiles, even the men,
whose boots have become quiet.
This man sees immediately
that the world he has made
is turned around here, or
better, that this is a test.
One more test to show what he is.
A real man is stronger
and remembers what he has been.
Himself, he feels no pain,
tries to feel no pain, no
flinch, speaks no words, gives
nothing so as to keep
from becoming less, weaker,
trying to keep all the parts
of himself, even from the priest.
He nods, simply, imagining
the priest as a man
caught in a party hat until dawn,
but dull anyway—he would not sing.
And then one day he lets himself
be tricked, agrees to be turned.
He is, after all, a father,

in his most secret life,
who must listen sometimes,
but only sometimes, to a woman,
to daughters who try to laugh.
Here finally he feels a pain.
And he wonders, one night, still
to himself, where does a young
man, a real man, wear his teeth?
What does he kill with his hands.

I Held His Name

In a room on a shelf away from everything else
she still kept his hats, in a row.
Everything in the room took care of him,
she did, the hats did, the dusted pictures of him
looking at it all without a smile.
And on Thursday nights when she did the dishes,
visiting, I would look at all of his heads
or the way his one head was so many places,
how in each of the hats it was still there.
I could see its shape, too big sometimes
in the weakest hats that right away had gone bad,
see where his uneven ears must have had on them
the unfair weight of the hat
and the sky and the night and the dreams.
In one hat I found the hair he went without.
This was where he must have lost it
and I took it with me without telling.
But he knew, and the next time I looked at the hats
nothing happened, so it was all right.
All of the days I spent there and the nights
she gave this man a name, but it did not work.
If he walked down the street I would have known him
by his head, by the way in my hands
on Thursday nights by myself I had held it
quick, but carefully, my hands just enough apart.
Sometimes off the shelf it would fall into my arms.
Sometimes because I wanted it to, sometimes
it fell as I hunted other things.